Identity Papers

Also by Ian Seed

Anonymous Intruder (Shearsman Books, 2009)
Shifting Registers (Shearsman Books, 2011)
Makers of Empty Dreams (Shearsman Books, 2014)

Chapbooks

No One Else at Home
    (translated from the Polish of Joanna Skalska) (Flax, 2007)
the straw which comes apart
    (translated from the Italian of Ivano Fermini) (Oystercatcher Press, 2010)
Amore mio (Flaxebooks, 2010)
Threadbare Fables (Like This Press, 2012)
Sleeping with the Ice Cream Vendor (Knives, Forks and Spoons Press, 2012)

Ian Seed

Identity Papers

Shearsman Books

First published in the United Kingdom in 2016 by
Shearsman Books
50 Westons Hill Drive
Emersons Green
BRISTOL
BS16 7DF

Shearsman Books Ltd Registered Office
30–31 St. James Place, Mangotsfield, Bristol BS16 9JB
(this address not for correspondence)

www.shearsman.com

ISBN 978-1-84861-470-3

ACKNOWLEDGEMENTS
My thanks to the editors of the following publications where some of
these poems have previously appeared: *The Bow-Wow Shop*;
The Café Irreal; Flash: The International Short-Short Story Magazine;
*Flax; The Fortnightly Review; Pandora's Box; PN Review; Poetry Salzburg
Review; Shearsman; Tears in the Fence*; and *Threadbare Fables*
(a Like This Press pamphlet).

Contents

'I thought my first wife lay on my left arm and somebody took her away from my side which made me wake up unhappy I thought as I awoke somebody said Mary but nobody was near—I lay down with my head towards the north to show my self the steering point in the morning.'

—John Clare

For Justyna and Chiara

I

Place to Rent

The concierge told us that the flat had been occupied by an old bachelor. We left our toddler daughter with her and made our way up the steep winding staircase to have a look. It was not what we expected. The walls were undecorated, and there were small jagged holes where the cold came through. A single steel bed without a mattress was the only piece of furniture. The air reeked of loneliness. My wife wanted to leave. But here was our daughter in the doorway. How had she climbed up the staircase without falling? How had she known where to find us?

In the Pavilion

After wandering around all morning, I sat down on an iron bench and fell asleep. I was woken by a young waitress asking me for my order.

'I hadn't even realised this part of the pavilion was a café,' I said.

She smiled invitingly. 'Wouldn't you like to try our lunchtime roast pork with apple sauce?' I couldn't refuse, although I knew my wife would be making a meal at home.

When I had eaten, a small, strangely-coloured bird appeared. It fluttered just above my forehead. I put the back of my hand out, partly to invite the bird to perch there, partly to ward it away from my face. But the bird just moved down and hovered near my lips as if it might find a crumb on them.

Only when the waitress arrived with the bill, did the bird fly away. I wondered if she could tell me what kind of bird it was, but she said she knew of no such thing in the pavilion.

Parenthood

I have just discovered that I have a son, now a grown man. While I wait at the station to meet him for the first time, I wonder how vulnerable he must have been growing up without his father.

But my son turns out to be a tall, strong woman. Over coffee she tells me that she makes her living as a priest and as a comedian. 'Everyone is full of such contradictions,' she says, 'but few of us have the joy of living them out.'

She makes me realise I no longer need to hide so much away. So I take my newfound son to my mother's house.

'My God, isn't she beautiful!' my mother says. Then she gives us the news that she herself is pregnant. Soon I will have a baby brother or sister.

News

Sitting on the back seat on the top deck of a double decker bus, I wonder how I shall announce the number of children my father had. I have to count on my fingers to remember. Sixteen in all! After his death I found out that he had a fourth family. His third family thought that they were the last, the chosen ones, that my father's first two families were just rehearsals to prepare the ground for them, his real family. How will they react when they find out the truth? And how will his fourth family feel when they learn of us? They are still children, while I am almost an old man. They live on the other side of town. I am on my way now to see them for the first time.

Affair

The storm was so strong it brought down the oak tree in my garden. Amongst its wreckage I found a bedraggled youth, who told me he had been living in the tree. Now he had nowhere to go. When I took him into my home, he was grateful, but showed no respect for the people in the village. He spent most of his time playing pranks on them.

One day he disappeared. As the weeks went by, I couldn't help hoping he would never return, even as I prayed for his well-being. When a naked body was found in the river, we all assumed it was his. Then one summer dawn I drew back the curtains of my French windows and found him hiding there. He wanted to know who I had been messing about with in his absence.

Honoured Guest

Walking with my wife and daughter in the park, I came across a small boy. He started throwing stones at us. I went up to him and grabbed his wrist. 'Where do you live?' I asked as gently as I could. To my surprise, he said he would show me. He took me down a hill to a small wood. He led me to a tin hut which he shared with his mother, grandmother and older sister. They invited me in, and made me a strong black tea. I remembered I had left my wife and daughter back in the park. I wondered if they would believe my story about the family in the tin hut.

The House that Jack Built

I entered the museum that contained the house that Jack built. The original purpose of the house had been to keep everyone out, and I thought that the game would be to find the secret door. I found instead a house without walls. A man with a strong, kind face was cooking broth on a stove for two boys in nightshirts, who had fallen asleep over a kitchen table. The scene looked warm and welcoming, yet I felt increasingly irritated by a faint waxen glow surrounding it. Moreover, ever since entering the museum I'd had the distinct sensation that the fingertips of my right hand were brushing against the bottom of someone's front teeth. I decided to have a word with the museum attendant.

Way Home

Because it's raining, I decide to try a shortcut I've never taken before. It's a path along a steep, wooded ridge. Halfway along, I see a line of men on horseback coming towards me. I step to one side to let them pass, but it's so slippery I have to grab a branch to stop myself from sliding down. The riders hardly notice. They only smile distantly at the sight of me holding on, splashed with mud from their horses' hooves.

Unspoken

At dinner, I wanted to ask my father about his experiences as a naval officer, but I was afraid to do so – he didn't like to talk about the war.

Just when I was about to speak, my mother said, 'Have you forgotten your sister Annabel? You never say anything about her.'

Annabel, my older sister, had drowned in the sea just a few months after I was born. My mother and father had been too busy fussing over me to see her slip away into the waves.

My mother reached out and took a photograph of Annabel from the sideboard. She put it to her ear as if it were a shell and the sea were whispering to her.

Discovery

When my mother was told she had cancer, my father managed to sprain his ankle. He seemed resentful that she was not well enough to look after him in the way she usually did. He was in a lot of pain, he shouted, propped up on pillows in bed. My mother took to sleeping in the spare bedroom. She gazed endlessly out of the window, a small girl about to set off on a great adventure alone.

New Teacher

The new teacher took us on a trip by double-decker bus. We were thrilled at first, but he kept telling us what we must and mustn't do. The children on the top deck were made to sing, while those on the bottom were not allowed to. We stopped at the side of the road for a toilet break when it was pouring with rain. The teacher told me to climb a nearby hill to try and gauge our exact position. It was so steep and slippery that I almost fell just as I reached the top. As I clung onto clumps of grass, I could hear the teacher and my classmates laughing. I didn't dare look down.

New Neighbours

Three men moved into the flat on the other side of the landing. They seemed a friendly bunch and would always greet me with smiles and loud helloes when we squeezed by one another on the narrow staircase. One of the three men was divorced and had a small daughter who would come to visit him. At first it seemed that the father and daughter had a special relationship. I could hear her calling 'Daddy' excitedly and his voice responding in warm, yet measured tones. I would watch through the window as she ran round the small lawn at the back and he stood there smiling proudly in his rolled-up shirtsleeves. But over the weeks I noticed his voice becoming harsher and more impatient. When he wanted her to come back into the house, he would take her hand and tug it roughly. I began to wonder if he was abusing her. It was as if he could sense my suspicions, for he would glare at me and say nothing whenever our paths crossed. Now the three men would shove by me on the stairs. They were always laughing at some joke that only they understood, but which I was sure was obscene.

Documentary

It's about a man recovering from mental health issues. We watch him as he opens the door of his sheltered housing bungalow, blinking in the sunlight. Next we see him attending a course at the local college. He waves cheekily at us through a classroom window, as if to say, 'Look! I'm trying to get better – all those taxes you pay for my treatment are not wasted.' But now he's walking on a sort of sea of crushed forest, formed from dead trees over millions of years. The sea heaves and swirls. He could be swallowed at any moment. Yet his smile radiates confidence.

Late

I drove too fast through the city because I was lost and wanted only to escape from its dangerous tangle of streets. Driving through a red traffic light, I almost knocked down a woman I hadn't seen for years.

She told me I should be more careful. Thanks to a careless driver, she had lost her only daughter. When I held her to comfort her, I didn't expect her body to be so warm and yielding. I was too old now to give her another child.

Pity

It was only through a chance meeting with an old acquaintance that I heard she was terminally ill. Over the years she had cut herself off from family and friends. I knew she lived in a small flat somewhere among the terraced houses on the edge of town. But it was much harder than I thought. All the houses seemed exactly alike. When I knocked on the doors, I was received only with blank and suspicious looks – as if I were bringing nothing but trouble with my desire to find someone who needed my help.

Cornered

The bike I've hired won't go any further up this steep cobbled street. I get off and push it, until I reach a series of low-hanging washing lines tied between the houses. Sheets, shirts and underwear block my way. A girl is weaving in and out of them with a dog which comes up to her shoulders. She throws a large stick covered in purple ribbons. It lands at my feet. When I pick the stick up, the dog jumps to wrestle it from me, playful yet determined. One by one, the ribbons come away. I see that it is not a stick, but a brownish bone, big enough to be a human femur. Now the girl is in front of me with her mother, who puts out a hand for me to give the bone back. Why do I still hold onto it so stubbornly?

Bright and Early

I got off the bus, thinking it was the stop for the sea. Instead I had stepped into an empty field. I walked across it and climbed a fence into another field. There was a girl crying. By her side were a discarded sketchbook and some scattered pieces of charcoal. 'This picture just won't come right,' she told me. I took her hand and kissed her face. Her skin was warm from the sun.

'You'll have to leave me here,' she said, at the gate to the farm where she lived, 'or there'll be too many questions.' I walked over more fields, hoping to come to the sea. I was sure I could hear its murmur somewhere in the distance. Instead, I arrived at a village by a river. It was already nightfall. An old woman took me in, letting me sleep in a hut in her garden. She said I would find what I was looking for if only I had faith.

In the coming months, the other villagers grew to accept me. Each night I knelt by my narrow bed and prayed until my knees were stiff and aching. Each morning I couldn't shake the weariness from my bones to get up and leave.

Patience

Returning home after my early morning walk, I found a cow standing alone on the pavement. She started to trot away, but then stopped and waited for me to approach, turning her eyes towards me. Attached to her bell was a flyer — an advertisement for an 'organic farm where animals are encouraged to be themselves'. There was also a phone number.

I knocked on my Polish neighbour's door to ask if he would ring the number while I kept an eye on the cow. But Mr Dudek was in no mood to help. After years of putting himself out for others, he said, he still had no money in the bank.

One or two faces were peeping at us now from bedroom windows. I went back to the cow and patted her spine. It was wet with dew.

2

Fitting In

There were postcard views of the river from the office. But in my new job I was an outsider from the provinces. I never ate lunch with my colleagues at the canteen tables, but instead went for walks down long corridors. Whenever I went past the desk of the HR man who'd hired me, his bald head would look up and he would stroke his reddish beard. He never spoke, but I could feel his gaze linger over me with wistful regret.

One stormy spring morning, the river flooded its banks. It rushed headlong into the office and carried us away, twisting and turning in its filthy brown water, through the streets of the city. I felt more comfortable now, less self-conscious, more like everybody else. A reddish beard floated its tendrils like torn away seaweed beside me.

Jane's Face

When Jane joined our company, we all — man and woman alike — fell in love with her. Never had we seen someone so beautiful. Yet she kept her distance from the start, and over the months our admiration turned to envy and resentment.

One time a company trip was organised for a hike along the coast. It was a cold and windy day, and there was no else around on the pebbled beach. Jane walked ahead of the rest of us. We began to whisper about how stuck up she was. Our voices grew louder and louder as we walked.

She turned towards us: 'You don't care about me. You're just obsessed with the way I look. But this face isn't mine. If you knew the truth, you would not want to get so close.'

And she reached up to her left temple with the nails of her right hand, and in one quick diagonal movement tore her beautiful face away. Underneath we could see another face scarred and disfigured.

'Yes,' she said, 'this is the real me. And now you, all of you, just reach up with your hand as I did and tear the mask away.'

Being True

I kept hanging around the town, even though I had lost my job. In particular I hung around a bar frequented by literary bohemian types, among them a vampish woman who dressed Goth-style and who was having an affair with a German publisher of experimental poetry. One evening at a party she pinned me to a wall and glued her lips to mine. I had no desire to escape — I had never been so expertly kissed in my life — but out of the corner of my eye, I could see the publisher getting more and more annoyed. He stood up, called for silence and gave a small speech, in which he quoted a German proverb to illustrate that the only life worth living was the one where you were true to the thing you loved. However, his translation into English didn't quite make sense. When I extricated myself from the woman and questioned him about the translation, he challenged me to a fight. I backed away and wandered off into the night. How could I ever persuade him to publish my book of poetry now? Some kind of animal followed me down the road. Because of the dark I couldn't see what it was, but it refused to be shaken off.

Employment

I had been out of work for some time. One morning a card was pushed under my door. On it was written: 'Africa re-emerging. Jobs available. Good money.' I gave them a call.

Successful applicants were invited to an introductory luncheon. The head hunter sat at the end of a long table. I was surprised at how smartly everyone was dressed. Was it just me who couldn't afford a suit? But the head hunter took off his jacket and hung it from the back of his chair. Soon everyone else did the same.

When it was time to stand up and give his speech, the head hunter spoke of the virtues of hard work, of not eating too much at a luncheon, and of always having a smile on our faces. He began complaining in a half-jokey sort of way about his new secretary, who, he said, was sulky and sloppy. We all smiled.

The secretary, who was next to me, shoved me with her elbow. She wanted me to pass her some left-over meat. I wanted to be unemployed again.

Work and Leisure

When I had been unemployed for over a year, the council found me a job in a local factory. I did my best to get on with my companions, to hide my education. But after just a few weeks, I was more productive than anyone. Soon I was spotted by the authorities and awarded a medal, which I was obliged to wear on my overalls.

On Saturdays I would take a bus into the city. I enjoyed listening to classical music on my CD player and watching the rain beat against the window close to my face. In the city was a multi-salon cinema where I could wander from one film to another. Sometimes I would fall asleep there. Once I was woken by a bunch of lads pouring a bottle of fizzy drink over my head. They ran away laughing. I couldn't find my CD player, and thought they must have stolen it. But later I found it next to my feet, hidden in the dark.

Changes

The floor in my flat was starting to slope. Meanwhile, the block next to ours was being demolished to make way for a chain pub and restaurant. For several months, the air was full of dust. When the pub was ready, an opening party was organised for local residents. They asked me to judge a competition there, but I found it hard to concentrate because I was worried about my floor, which by this time was sloping so much it was impossible to stay in one place without sliding down it.

Communal Spirit

A pack of abandoned dogs started roaming the fields at the back of our street. One sunny morning, a group was organised to clear up all the shit they left behind. Special plastic bags were distributed and we began our task. No one seemed to realise that the problem would only get worse unless we offered a home to the dogs. At lunchtime, we sat down on the grass with our full bags. Already the dogs were making a mess again, but most people were now tucking into sandwiches they had brought along as a picnic. I wished I'd done the same. A neighbour I didn't like put a hand on my shoulder sympathetically.

Ramblers

It was a cold dry day. We were out walking over forest-covered hills. There was a man from India with us who spoke little English, but who kept smiling. He carried an old sack over his shoulder. Like his smile, his sack made us suspicious, but we didn't ask him what was inside. When we stopped in a clearing to eat our sandwiches, he gathered some twigs and lit a fire. While we watched, afraid yet curious, he opened the sack and brought out a pot and ladle. With just a few ingredients and water, he had soon made a spicy, sweet-smelling broth. I was the first to try it. Thus, he won his way into my heart, for it was like nothing I had ever tasted before.

Boss

It'd been a tough morning at work. I went to a bar and ordered a coffee with liquor. I had just sat down when my boss walked in. I hastily took out a memo from my briefcase and pretended to study it.

My boss smiled and sat down next to me. Without a word he dropped a memo of his own on the table for me to read. It was written by his solicitor to the two tenants of a house he owned nearby, threatening them with eviction unless they paid for the bed they had broken. It was as if he wished to impress upon me that it was this kind of power that counted, not doing one's petty duty at work.

'Buying and renting out properties is a good way to make money,' I said, although I had never done anything of the sort in my life.

'It's the only way these days,' he assented.

I started to tell him about my own days as a tenant. I had always treated properties with respect. But I stopped when I realised he was fiddling round with his laptop and not listening. God knows what they had been doing in that bed, I wondered, with some envy.

Gift

In my youth I often stayed in other people's houses, sleeping on their couch or floor if there wasn't a spare bed. I didn't have the money to pay rent, but I would always leave a few coins behind when I left. Years later when I had a house of my own, I bumped into a friend who had once put me up for a few days. He still had the coins, he told me. Would I like them back now, as a gift?

Worlds

In the newspaper office I listen to the spiel about immigrants invading our towns. I say nothing in protest – I am here for a job interview, after all.

In the meantime, my landlord has moved a Romanian family into the house where I have been living on my own. At first I am glad of the company. They are so friendly. Soon, however, they are playing loud music, shouting up and down the stairs, and blocking the drive with two brash cars.

The father is warm and hearty. Each evening he claps me on the back and invites me to eat and drink with them. I yearn for a corner to be lonely in.

Bond

When I had to move to take on a temporary job, I rented a cheap room in a single mum's house. Over the weeks, a bond grew between her small son and me. He loved it when I picked him up and twirled him round. Afterwards, he would lay his head in the crook of my arm. His mum said she would never have believed her son could connect with a man in this way after the abuse he had suffered at the hands of his father.

My job came to an end. It was time for me to leave. The boy wouldn't stop crying. In the end, his mother said, I had betrayed his trust and was no better than his father.

Outlook

The head manager of the government buildings where I worked summoned me to his office. He told me with a fixed smile that I had half an hour to make a decision: either to join the new Green Movement or to be made redundant. He gave me a form to take away with me to fill in. Back at my desk, I saw a female colleague filling out the same form. She complained that it gave her a terrible headache. When I offered to massage her temples, she refused, saying that I would only take advantage of her. Too many men had made promises in the past, she told me, including the head manager. She didn't see why I should be any different.

Desertion

The two women at my door wore Salvation Army hats. I had promised them some money, apparently. It was raining, but I couldn't invite them in because I had to dash to meet my lover for our weekly rendezvous in a hotel.

Later I saw the two women in the hotel foyer. One of them pointed at me, but I was able to jump into a lift just as its doors were closing.

In the upstairs corridor, I bumped into my old boss, who was there for a conference.

'Have you seen those two Salvation Army women?' he asked. 'They wanted money from me.'

Things were not going so well at work, he went on. It was a shame I had left my job with the business in such a mess.

Ways

The girl next door let me kiss her in spite of the risk a neighbour might spot us. With my tongue I wrote the alphabet on her clitoris until she came and turned over to offer me the softness of her behind. I thought of the tubes which climb the wall of the Beaubourg Centre in Paris, of how, from the inside, they must make an impossible maze. How should I know which way to go? Who might I meet on turning a corner?

Leak

There's a beautiful girl who keeps pursuing me, but I prefer the melancholy and easy intimacy of my wife. One evening when I'm on my own at home, I hear the girl calling me from the street outside. At the same time, it starts to rain. The rain becomes so heavy, it leaks in through the ceiling. Why didn't my wife and I sort this out when we still had the money to do so? And why hasn't she come back home yet? It's almost time for me to lock everything up and go to sleep.

Riposte

We were both students in the same class. There was a complicity between us, an understanding that we would help each out if we got stuck. One day when she asked me a simple question, I found that I could not stop my reply from becoming more and more complex. It became a long poetic text of strange beauty that even I could not understand. It wanted not to find an answer, but to create more questions. It wanted openings. My friend leant forward, put a finger to her lips and started to unbutton her blouse. 'I'll teach you about openings,' she whispered, filling me with panic.

In the Park

I bumped into the man who'd had an affair with my wife and who happened to be an external examiner for the university where I worked. He was out walking his dog. We sat down together on a bench outside a closed cafe and he put his hand on my arm. He told me that he held both my wife and I in equally high esteem. It started to drizzle as he spoke. His dog rolled onto its back on the muddy path. She wants you to tickle her tummy, he told me.

3

Invitation

Although I hardly knew them, they invited me to dinner at their villa. Perhaps they wanted to practise their English with me, as well as try to make me feel at home in their country.

The husband and I stood by the French windows sipping a glass of white wine, while his wife went to look for a record she wanted me to hear.

'What a beautiful view,' I said, feeling that this was the right thing to say about the villas dotting the hillside across the river.

His wife returned with the record. 'La négresse,' she said, placing it on the turntable and lifting the needle. 'You won't have heard anything so divine.'

I looked out again at the river. A fisherman had arrived and was casting his line onto the water. I wished I could be with him, even though I had never been fishing in my life.

Differences

I was already middle-aged and divorced when I was sent to Italy. An Italian family was paid to put me up until I could find a place of my own. They were suspicious of me at first, although the father was friendly in a gruff sort of way. All I wanted to do was to fit in, to be one of them.

A woman from England arrived to work in my office as a translator. She was fresh out of university. The father made jokes about a future wife for me, though I was obviously much older than her. I was going bald and grey, unlike the father. He had a head of rich, dark, wavy hair, which looked especially beautiful when ruffled by a breeze in the Italian sunlight.

Tram in Milan

It was an old tram, one of those with wooden seats and floor from the 1930s. The conductress walked down the narrow aisle selling tickets. Her dyed black hair, false eyelashes and bright lipstick accentuated her age. There was an air about her which was both flirtatious and officious.

She reached me as I was standing by the door, ready to get off. However, I had pressed the bell too late and the tram was already moving on. Now I would have to pay more.

'I pressed the bell for the last stop,' I told her, trying to charm her with a smile and my English accent.

'Too late now,' she said, pursing her lips. Perhaps she remembered me from the week before when I'd left the tram without paying.

'You should have a little more faith in people,' I said, dropping the coins carelessly into her hand.

She replied in a torrent of Milanese dialect. Everyone on the tram turned to stare. When the doors opened, I jumped out and tried to disappear in the passing crowd.

Journey South

My train from Milan is due to leave in a few minutes. I go into a bar to buy an espresso, but I have no coins, only a 50,000-euro note. The smart barman lets me pay with that, but then no one brings me either my espresso or my change. When I ask for my money back, the barman shrugs as if to say he has no idea what I am talking about. I take out my wallet and show him its empty inside. The barman reaches under the counter and comes up with a fistful of Italian lira which looks old enough to predate the Second World War. He offers it to me as if I were a beggar.

Another Tram

Dressed in my best jacket and jeans, I'm on my way to meet an Italian girl. One of my high school students gets onto the tram and asks me where I'm going.

'You need to dress more coolly,' he says. 'You look too English.'

'I do all right,' I say.

'How many Italian women have you had?' he challenges.

I shake my head and smile, but he misinterprets me: 'Look, if you're that hard up, why not try a dating site. At the very least, you'll find a foreign woman.'

I say nothing. How can I tell him that this is 1983? I'm still a young man and no one is using the internet.

Incident

I'm sitting with Scotch Dave in a bar in Milan. In a couple of hours we'll be on our way home, taking the midnight train to Paris, and from there to London. The bar's filling up with smartly-dressed Italians out on a Friday night. We must look odd with our battered rucksacks and unshaven faces.

Some girls sit at our table – there's nowhere else for them. To my surprise, one of the prettiest starts talking to Dave. She seems fascinated by the fact that he's from Scotland. But when a burly youth comes over, she quickly loses interest. In any case, it's time for us to head to the station.

Halfway down the street we realise we are being followed by a small crowd. The youth taps Dave on the shoulder. Dave's response is a punch so clumsy it doesn't even connect. I hear the crack of the youth's fist on Dave's jaw. Shouting that we have a train to catch, I rush into the melee to pull Dave away. Now the youth squares up to me, egged on by his companions.

I have the sense that we are all on a film set, that this whole scene is for the benefit of an audience as yet invisible.

Russian Bar in Turin

It's a place I have just stumbled upon, yet I've been living here for years. I order a red-coloured drink whose name I mispronounce. The barman sniggers. In a corner, a big Russian man is holding forth to some Italians. In Russia, he says, under communism, at least everyone had a job. The Italians nod like children. It's then that I notice the red flag with hammer and sickle on the wall behind him. Speaking of the necessity of every individual joining the Revolution, the Russian flips a beer mat into the air, and gestures for me to catch it. The Italians watch me expectantly.

Mean-Spirited

I met up with Nunzia, my ex, when I went back to Turin one week on business. She was a wife and mother now, I was a husband and father. We went to the bar where we used to sit in a dark corner on a Friday night. It was still the same bartender, much older. Without asking, he made us our favourite cocktail. 'Just like it used to be,' Nunzia said. I smiled in agreement, though I thought it tasted much weaker than the one I remembered.

Filer à l'anglaise

At an Italian bookfair, I met two authors, a man and a woman. They read out to a small audience clustered around one of the stalls. As a foreigner, I felt obliged to show generosity and buy one of their books, but they were expensive, and when I flicked through their pages, I could see how dull and difficult they were. I decided to sneak away without buying anything. A back path took me to a high, steep bank leading up to a busy road. I climbed the bank and almost fell at the top because the edge of the road was crumbling away due to recent floods. Luckily, there was a branch I could grab hold of. However, once on the road, I could see just how dangerous it was, with cars coming at top speed in both directions, and no path for pedestrians. Yet I could not face going back to the fair, for now down below I could see some of the crowd pointing up at me, including the two authors whose books I didn't want.

Mix-up

A child was murdered in a house in Italy. I had left something in that house when I visited it for my research on the famous Italian author, Giuseppe Scala, who had died of a heart attack shortly after my conversation with him just before his fortieth birthday. I remembered him weeping when I told him his books were responsible for changing my life.

Later, my wife and I were approached by the Italian police. It was clear we had nothing to do with the death of either the child or the author, but they wanted to know if we had noticed anything strange. They took the liberty of commenting on my wife's beauty and intelligence. It was a rare combination, they told me. That evening, we went to a restaurant they had recommended. My wife, who was a linguist, got cross with the waiter for bringing us our dessert before the main dish. 'It's like getting the past perfect mixed up with the past simple,' she said. I was more annoyed with him for the way he responded with silent disdain.

Midway

The city on the hill was further away than I expected. Each time I thought I was nearly there, I realised I had only reached the top of a brow. I considered going back down to the village where I had stayed the night before, but it would soon be dark. By the time I reached the outskirts of the city, all the shutters of the houses were closed, with just one or two lights shining behind them. I came to a piazza. Some men with their shirt sleeves rolled up were sitting at a table outside a closed bar and playing cards. The smell of cigarettes filled the air. I walked up to them and asked in Italian if they knew of an inn where I could spend the night. But they only shrugged, shook their heads and carried on playing cards as if I wasn't there. I decided it might be better to find somewhere to camp down in the woods just outside the city. As I walked away, one of the men cursed and another laughed.

Refuge

I came to this country because everyone said it was beautiful and peaceful. But now as I climb a hill in the sunshine, the sounds of a street battle reach me from the town below.

Just nearby is an infants' school. Perhaps I will be safer there. Through the window I can see some kind of award ceremony taking place. Two small girls are being presented with bouquets of flowers. I decide to pick some wild ones from a hedgerow as an extra gift for them.

When I open the door to the hall, all goes quiet. First the Director, then the children turn to stare at the flowers hanging from my hands. The Director shakes her head. 'So unnecessary,' she says. The children regard me sadly.

Ledge

Because of the train strike, I was stuck in a small mountain town. The woman in a dark blue uniform behind the kiosk window could give me only the vaguest information about how long the strike would last. She offered to alter my train ticket to make it valid for another month, though she warned me that this would be a forgery. I walked out of the station and climbed a hill by the railway line. As evening fell, I sat on a rock ledge, where I could see all the way down the valley and watch the sea darkening. I would have looked odd on my own up there to anyone passing by in a train below. But all the trains were frozen elsewhere.

Therapeutic Massage

When Nunzia told me she'd met someone else, I couldn't help it – I cried. She put her arms around me, but I could sense the disgust mingled with her pity. After that, I heard she'd left town with her new, rich boyfriend.

Years later I was walking through the annual trade fair that was held in the piazza when I saw Nunzia at a stall advertising *Massaggi terapeutici*. She looked a little plumper, her lower lip sagged, and the make-up around her eyes couldn't hide the wrinkles. Next to her was a small, balding man in what looked like a doctor's white coat. Behind them was a closed-off section under canvas.

'Are you sure this is a good idea?' Nunzia asked.

We stood under the canvas together hidden from view.

'It's nothing personal,' I said. 'I just need to get rid of my stress.'

I took off my shirt and lay front down on the narrow bed. She put her hands on me, worked her fingers down my spine. I was afraid I might cry again. Instead, I found myself ejaculating. After my ten minutes were up, I paid and left. On the way out, I was given a card by the balding man. In fancy lettering, it announced the imminent opening of an 'alternative health' clinic, but there was no address.

In the months that followed, I wandered the town in search of the place. One evening in a backstreet near the station, I came across a notice on yellowing paper in a small window: *Massaggi*. Nunzia wasn't there, neither was the balding man. And it was clear that this was not a clinic. But the woman who answered the door had a gentle face and I accepted her invitation to come in. After that, I went back on a weekly basis. It was not always the same woman who came to the door, but that didn't matter. Each time I closed my eyes, I could imagine that the hands on my body were Nunzia's.

Suspect

I was walking along the beach at Rapallo, when I saw her sitting on a towel, looking out at the flat grey sea. She had a tattoo of a snake on her thigh.

'Don't you remember me?' she said.

I wasn't sure that I did, but I sat down beside her, letting my thigh rest against the snake on hers.

It was then that I noticed the corner of an envelope sticking out of the sand. Pulling the sand away, I found a heap of envelopes, all with different names and addresses.

'How on earth did these get here?' I asked.

She looked at me rather than at the envelopes and raised her eyebrows. 'I don't know, but I think it's a matter for the police. Wouldn't you agree?' She spoke as if she suspected that it was me who had buried the envelopes there.

Find

The postman arrives with a leather-soled shoe which I must have left behind in my old flat years ago. Who found it and sent it on to me? It's almost unworn. Somewhere, I know, I still have the other shoe.

Volunteer

The woman at the kiosk has reserved a table seat for me. That will give me room to stretch my long legs, she says. She shows me on a diagram where the seat is.

'But it's not facing in the direction of the train,' I say.

'That's all we have available,' she says. 'Just be grateful you're not like him.' She points to a homeless man sitting on a bench nearby.

'I used to help homeless people,' I tell her.

Impressed by this, the man follows me all the way through the station to the train. He gets on after me and sits opposite me at the table. A mother and daughter move away to another seat.

A Meeting

In my rush, I'd taken the wrong train back up north. It was pitch black outside and I was afraid that the ticket inspector would fine me more than I could afford or throw me off the train. A stranger sat opposite me. 'A penny for your thoughts,' he said. I felt his gaze wander over my face and body, but didn't dare to raise my head to meet it. It was unpleasant, and yet made me feel that I mattered to someone. Before long, the ticket inspector could be seen at the far end of the carriage. Abruptly, the stranger got up and made for the toilet, leaving a manila folder on the table. The inspector – a kind-looking man with white hair, rimless spectacles and an old-fashioned inspector's cap – did not charge me any extra. He only told me that I would need to change trains at X, a small station in the middle of nowhere. To my surprise, he then picked up the manila folder and spilled its contents onto the table. It was clear from these that the stranger had stolen the personal details of people who had died in horrible circumstances. The inspector placed the contents back into the folder and passed on without saying a word. When the stranger returned to his seat, I made no mention of what had happened. I was trembling with fear, and yet when he offered to share a bottle of red wine with me, I accepted after only the slightest hesitation.

Offer

When I wake, we have arrived at a small, deserted station. It is already dark. An old man, who looks like a farmer, is sitting opposite me. I ask him when we will arrive at X.

He smiles. 'Oh, that was a long time ago. You've been asleep for hours.'

I wonder if I should get off while I still can and wait for a train back, even if it means spending the night in the station.

As if reading my thoughts, the old man says, 'There's some time yet. Why don't you join me for a drink down the road?' He gestures through the train window into the darkness in what I take to be the direction of a pub.

'All right, but just for one,' I say.

I have heard that the beer this far north is very strong. I need to keep my wits about me if I am ever going to make it home.

4

The Gift

I hadn't bought my father a birthday present in years. I usually made do with a card, but this year he was going to Japan on a business trip. I went to a Japanese shop just off Piccadilly Circus. There was a model of a black steam train in the window. My father had been crazy about trains all his life, but when I picked it up and held it in my hands, it felt small and childish. There had to be something else I could buy. On the wall was a calendar with water-colour designs and dates in both Japanese and English. This would be useful, but then again he might find it boring. I looked around the shop. So much to choose from, I didn't know where to begin. When he died two days later, regret was mixed with relief that I no longer needed to buy him anything at all.

The Right Way

There was no one else on the narrow road that ran along the high ridge. You insisted on stopping the car to take one last look at the woods below, before they merged into the greying light.

'We'll miss the funeral,' I said.

'We'll have missed it now, anyway,' you said.

We were not even sure we had come the right way. I imagined them all leaving the cemetery in small groups, perhaps wondering for a moment where we were, why we hadn't come. I only realised then how many years had passed since the last time I'd seen them.

'Perhaps there's still time,' I said.

But you sat there in silence, admiring the colours of the vanishing sun, as if I hadn't spoken.

Shapes Which Console

The innkeeper's tale ends where it begins – a joke about a woman when what I wanted was a bedtime story of angels. He unbuttons his greasy waistcoat, stands closer to the fire, watches us with small, bright eyes.

Our card game has its adventures. As we play, we see the light from the flames change on our sleeves and hands, telling of possibilities we won't remember when we return to our day jobs. Surely it's time to go, but her stockinged knees press against mine as the icy night presses on the window.

When I lift my tankard to my lips, it leaves a blurred ring on the table. I'm trying in vain to restore a face to my mind. The innkeeper has suggestions for a new game, but no one is listening. He really could be anyone at all.

B & B

The exercise book was full of my own writings, a mixture of the banal and beautiful. I showed it to the radio broadcaster and poet P., who happened to be staying in the same B&B. I explained to him that this was how I wrote – lots of writing, then picking out the images and lines that appealed to me. He flicked through the pages, got up and walked away with it. Should I go after him? There might be some things in the book that were too revealing. On the other hand, he was in a position to promote my writing. I decided to take my cup of coffee up to my room to mull over the situation. Just as I reached my door, I heard the B&B owner calling to me from the bottom of the stairs. What on earth did I think I was doing? Drinks were to be consumed in the dining area only.

The Poet

'You're starting to lose your hair.'

'Never mind about that,' I tell her. 'Come and have a look at these.'

There are sheets of unsigned handwritten poems pinned to the department noticeboard. They are almost indecipherable. Someone taps me on the shoulder. It's the poet P., my academic supervisor. It turns out the poems are his.

'You'll be hearing these at the reading tonight,' he announces, assuming that we are going.

It turns out to be a small audience. We sit on the front row to keep him happy. I close my eyes. He will think I do so to savour his words. In reality, I am wondering if the people behind me can see the beginnings of my bald patch.

His Eyes Closed

I thought he was indifferent to all of us around him, concerned solely with his own singing and the music of his pain, but when I decided to stop listening, a message was brought to me outside the auditorium that he was angry at my leaving and was waiting, songless, for my return.

Identity Papers

Back in the country where I used to live as a very young man, I went to visit the house where I'd once rented a room. A dowdy-looking woman answered the door. It was only when I noticed the tiny mole on her nose that I realised she was the pretty girl who used to play in the hallway.

She had no idea who I was. I took out my yellowed ID papers, showed her the ancient photo of my face with the local police stamp on it. Still she was hesitant. I reminded her of how she used to tease me because of the way I spoke their language. A smile flickered across her face. There was a letter still waiting for me, she said, tucked away in the back of a drawer somewhere. It must have arrived shortly after I left all those years ago. She went to look for it while I waited on the step.

When she returned, I was surprised at how untouched the envelope looked. I recognized the handwriting on the front as my father's. I started to open it, forgetting it was too late to reply.

Expat

It was just growing light. I was walking back to my Paris flat from the metro. Someone sprang at me from a doorway and tried to grab my wallet from my pocket. More than frightened, I was ashamed that he'd dared to attack me, for he was only a scrawny youth and, though his eyes were vicious, his lips were pretty and feminine. I grabbed him round the neck and wrestled him to the ground. The smell of his sweat was sweet. I held his trembling body against mine until the police arrived.

Later, the French authorities requested that he trim the roses in the courtyard belonging to the block of flats where I lived. This would form part of his rehabilitation. I watched him closely the first time. The smell of his sweat mingled with that of the cut stems. I pointed out to him a rose he'd missed. His face took on a petulant, offended look. He finished his task and left. I was about to chase after him with the vague idea of making amends, when a head poked out of a window.

'Bonjour, monsieur!' the head called out. This was an old man, a gossip. No doubt he had something to say about the youth. I hurried away, even though I knew that my neighbour would tell everyone I was no more than an oafish Englishman.

Trial

She's still not safe. The criminal gang who robbed and assaulted her have threatened to kill her family if she doesn't drop the charges. I try to reassure her. Surely they will understand that the consequences for murder would be even greater. But she won't stop crying.

'I will talk to these thugs and sort it out,' I say.

All day I go wandering through the city in search of them. I find their house at the edge of a lake. Bathed in light reflected from the water, it is so beautiful that I forget what it is I came here for. If only I could stop my thoughts from floating around, I tell myself, as I walk away up a steep street towards the setting sun.

Roles

President Obama was staying at hotel where I worked as a security guard. He finished his crab sandwich and coffee, and asked if I would go and get him another. I was happy to oblige, but at the bar they put it on my bill, not his. A little later, some clowns on stilts came into the foyer. They were collecting for charity, they said. They made me feel small because I no longer had any money to give them.

Trick

Hurrying to the station to catch my train home, I realised I'd taken a wrong turning. I was at the back of a church. The quickest way now would be to go through it. I went in by a door in the corner. After the busy streets, the inside of the church seemed to envelop me with its silence. At the bottom of some steps, was a statue of the bleeding Christ. As I came near, I saw it was a man dressed up. He thrust a palm in front of me and glared. Just for a few coins, I thought, and walked on. 'That's right,' I heard him mutter behind me. I thought of turning round and taking issue with him. But this was a church. Besides, I was only passing through.

November

I was sitting on a park bench, thinking of an old friend, of how I had never embraced him. I hadn't seen him for years, and yet as I was wondering about him, I saw him pass by in the light rain that had started to fall. He turned and stared as if he could not believe it was really me. He seemed to have hardly changed, while I had aged almost beyond recognition. I got up and ran to take him in my arms, to hold him so close I could stop his eyes from wandering over my face.

Man

After many countries, I came across him by a stream at the edge of the desert. I didn't know at first that I had met him before – as a hunchback by a fire under a bridge, as a woman wandering through foggy streets, as a child in a doorway with palm outstretched, as a wounded animal I never learnt the name of. Each time I had walked away, afraid. Yet he was smiling as if glad to see me. With a small gesture, he invited me to sit beside him and bathe my face. And I realised then who he was, and that nothing was too late after all.

Lightning Source UK Ltd.
Milton Keynes UK
UKOW04f1234030216

267656UK00004B/68/P